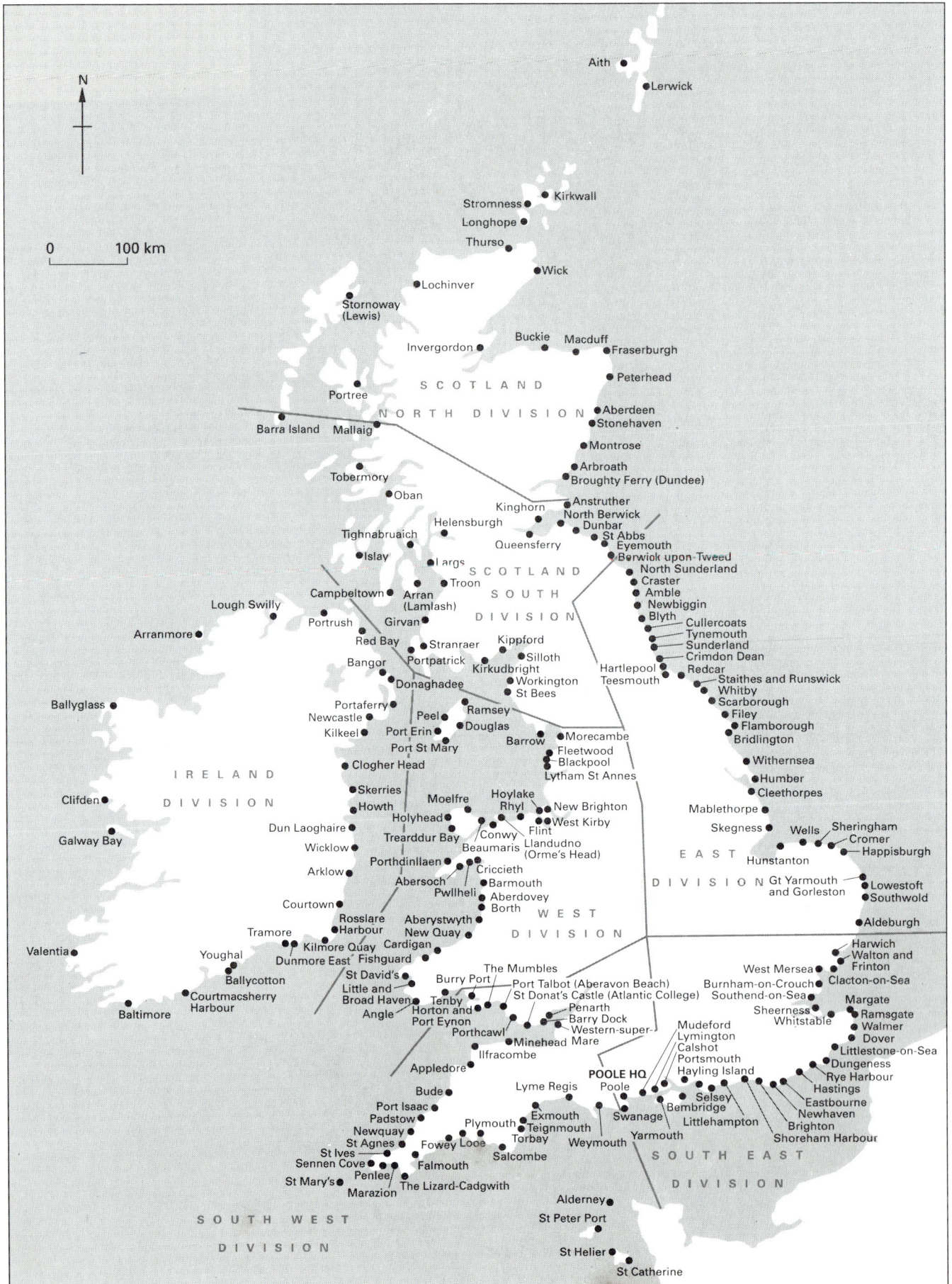

Aith
Lerwick

Kirkwall
Stromness
Longhope
Thurso
Wick
Lochinver
Stornoway (Lewis)
Buckie Macduff
Invergordon Fraserburgh
SCOTLAND Peterhead
Portree
NORTH DIVISION Aberdeen
Barra Island Mallaig Stonehaven
Montrose
Tobermory Arbroath
Oban Broughty Ferry (Dundee)
Kinghorn Anstruther
Helensburgh North Berwick
Tighnabruaich Queensferry Dunbar
Islay SCOTLAND St Abbs
Largs Eyemouth
SOUTH Berwick upon Tweed
Campbeltown Arran Troon North Sunderland
(Lamlash) DIVISION Craster
Lough Swilly Girvan Amble
Portrush Newbiggin
Arranmore Red Bay Stranraer Kippford Blyth Cullercoats
Bangor Portpatrick Silloth Tynemouth
Donaghadee Kirkudbright Sunderland
Ballyglass Workington Crimdon Dean
Portaferry St Bees Hartlepool Redcar
Newcastle Peel Ramsey Teesmouth Staithes and Runswick
Kilkeel Port Erin Douglas Whitby
Clifden Port St Mary Barrow Morecambe Scarborough
IRELAND Fleetwood Filey
Galway Bay DIVISION Clogher Head Blackpool Flamborough
Lytham St Annes Bridlington
Skerries Moelfre Hoylake Withernsea
Howth Rhyl New Brighton Humber
Holyhead West Kirby Cleethorpes
Dun Laoghaire Conwy Flint Mablethorpe
Valentia Trearddur Bay Beaumaris Llandudno Skegness Wells Sheringham
Wicklow (Orme's Head) Cromer
Porthdinllaen Criccieth EAST Happisburgh
Arklow Barmouth Hunstanton
Abersoch Pwllheli Aberdovey DIVISION Gt Yarmouth Lowestoft
Courtown Borth and Gorleston Southwold
WEST
Rosslare Aberystwyth DIVISION Aldeburgh
Tramore Harbour New Quay
Kilmore Quay Cardigan Harwich
Youghal Dunmore East Fishguard Walton and
Ballycotton St David's West Mersea Frinton
Courtmacsherry Little and Burry Port Burnham-on-Crouch Clacton-on-Sea
Baltimore Harbour Broad Haven Port Talbot (Aberavon Beach) Southend-on-Sea
Tenby St Donat's Castle (Atlantic College) Margate
Angle Horton and Penarth Sheerness Ramsgate
Port Eynon Barry Dock Whitstable Walmer
Porthcawl Western-super- Dover
Minehead Mare Mudeford Littlestone-on-Sea
Ilfracombe Lymington Dungeness
POOLE HQ Calshot Rye Harbour
Appledore Lyme Regis Poole Portsmouth Hastings
Hayling Island Eastbourne
Bude Exmouth Swanage Selsey Newhaven
Port Isaac Bembridge Brighton
Padstow Plymouth Teignmouth Weymouth Yarmouth Littlehampton Shoreham Harbour
Newquay Torbay
St Agnes Fowey Looe SOUTH EAST
St Ives Salcombe
Sennen Cove Falmouth DIVISION
St Mary's Penlee
Marazion The Lizard-Cadgwith
SOUTH WEST Alderney
St Peter Port
DIVISION
St Helier
St Catherine

Where is your nearest lifeboat station?

Rescue!

Book of the Sea

Nicola Baxter

Contents

Watts Books
London • New York • Sydney

All at sea

The English Channel is one of the busiest stretches of water in the world – but perhaps not quite as busy as this! Here are just some of the thousands of different vessels, people and objects that can be seen afloat around the coasts of Britain.

Can you spot the following?

A powerful tug pulling an oil-drilling platform to its final position in the North Sea.

A car ferry bringing vehicles and passengers from France.

A buoy marking a dangerous submerged wreck.

A container ship carrying goods from Belgium.

A fishing boat heading out to the fishing grounds.

A dredger keeping the deep-water channels into the harbour open.

A pilot boat taking a pilot out to an incoming oil tanker.

A yacht towing a dinghy.

Two power boats racing each other.

A submarine waiting outside the harbour.

A cabin cruiser coming in for more provisions.

A cross-Channel swimmer with her support vessel.

Finally, did you spot the windsurfer in difficulties a good way from the shore? Luckily someone has rung the coastguard, and an inshore RNLI lifeboat is about to be launched.

Covering the coast

Nowhere in Britain is more than 75 miles from the sea, so you are unlikely to be much further than that from your nearest lifeboat station. The 210 RNLI lifeboat stations cover almost the whole coast of Britain and Ireland. Of these, 182 operate all the year round, while the remaining 27 are open from March to October – the busiest time of the year for lifeboat services. Thirteen different classes of lifeboat are in service at the moment, but the fleet is updated constantly. There is a lifeboat to suit any kind of shore or harbour and the different sea conditions around the coast. What class of lifeboat is there at your nearest lifeboat station? There may be more than one!

The first of the 'fast lifeboats', the Waveney was developed from an American coastguard design, and lies afloat at moorings. She will be replaced by one of the new FABs.

The Tyne is an all-weather boat that can be launched from a slipway or lie afloat.

The Thames is designed to lie afloat. It may also be replaced by one of the FAB designs.

Designed to be launched from a slipway, only a few Solents now remain.

All-weather lifeboat designed to lie afloat on a mooring, the Arun will be replaced by one of the new Fast Afloat Boats (FABs) now being developed.

A lifeboat that can lie afloat at moorings, the Brede is designed for speed, and can operate in all but the most severe weather conditions.

Designed to be launched from a carriage, the Mersey is the most recent boat to go into service, and will replace Rother and Oakley class lifeboats.

The fast C Class inflatables are used for inshore service and are launched manually or from special trolleys or trailers.

The Atlantic 21 is known as a 'B Class' boat. Launched from carriages or slipways, Atlantics are fast inflatables with a rigid hull for inshore duties.

Launched manually or from a special trolley, the D Class inflatable is the smallest boat in the fleet.

5

The restless sea

Britain and Ireland are surrounded on every side by the sea, but this great body of water is never still. The unpredictable weather brings about some of this motion, but a great deal of the movement of the sea is caused by the tides, which can be predicted much more accurately.

Tides are caused by the gravitational pull of the moon and sun on the water of the oceans. This pull causes the water to rise and fall in a regular pattern. This happens over the whole sea, but it is usually only noticeable where the sea meets the land.

When the water is rising it is called a **flood tide**. When it is falling it is called an **ebb tide**. The time between the highest point of one flood tide and the next is about 12 hours and 25 minutes.

In some places the difference between high and low tide may be very dramatic. These pictures were taken at the same spot six hours apart.

Low tide (John Dodds Studios)

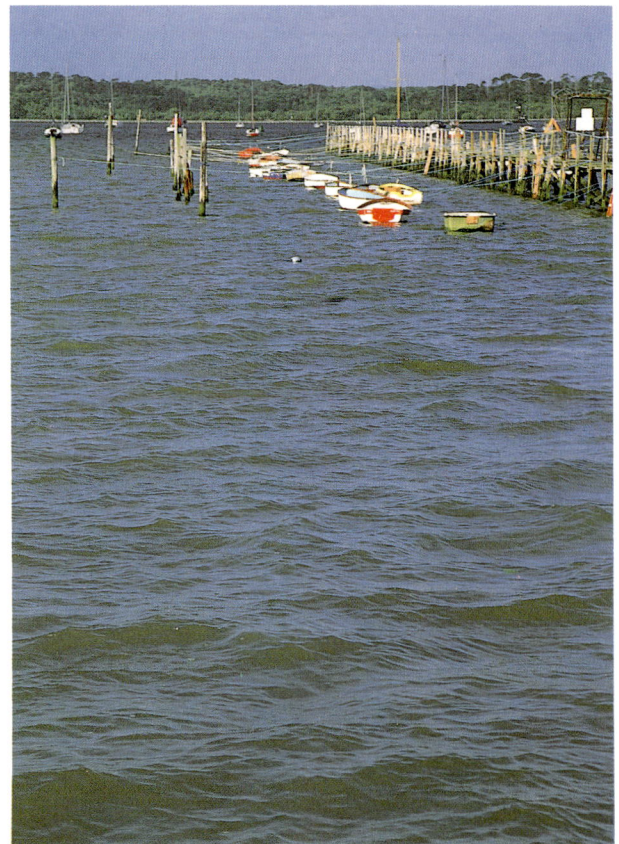

High tide (John Dodds Studios)

Although tides are regular in their rising and falling, some of them are higher or lower than others. This is also caused by the moon and sun. When the sun, moon and earth are in a straight line, there is a **spring tide**, which is higher than usual. When the moon and sun form a right angle to the earth, there is a **neap tide**, which is lower than usual. Despite their name, spring tides happen twice every month, as do neap tides.

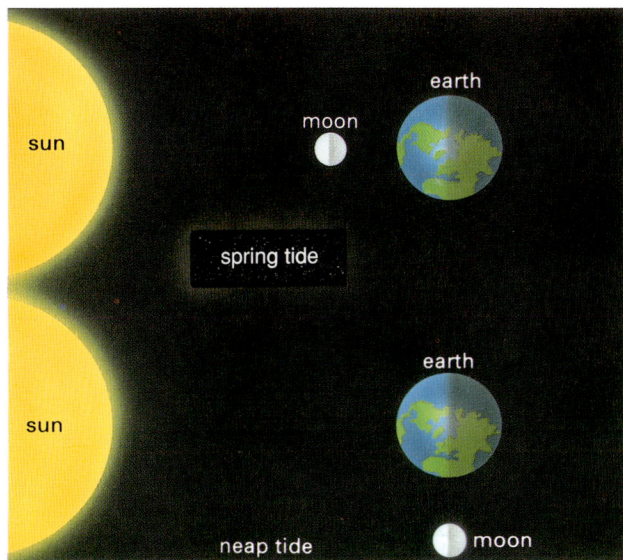

Headland surrounded by turbulent water
(Robin Sharp)

A buoy or a rock sticking out of the sea can sometimes tell you which way the tide is flowing. If the buoy has a 'wake', the tide is flowing in the same direction as the wake.

Did you know?

The sea covers 71% of the surface of the earth.

The rhythmic pattern of the tides also causes tidal streams.

Sometimes these are called currents. Water in a tidal stream moves faster than the water around it. This often happens around headlands and can be dangerous for swimmers and people in boats.

All on board

Lifeboat crews never know what situations they may be called upon to face – they must be ready for anything. As well as the permanent fixtures and fittings of a lifeboat, a great deal of other equipment has to be stowed away carefully in the boat. Anything that might be needed to save a life must be readily to hand, but there is no space on a lifeboat for unnecessary extras! Here you can see just some of the items that lifeboats carry.

Stores department at RNLI HQ
(John Dodds Studios)

Any lifeboat equipment that is used needs to be replaced quickly – there may be only minutes before a lifeboat is called out on duty again. The stores at RNLI Headquarters in Poole have thousands of different items of equipment ready to be rushed to the coast.

Every piece of equipment must be stowed in its proper place so that it can be found in seconds if needed. An item that is not safely stowed away may fall out of position and affect the lifeboat's ability to roll upright when capsized.

Storing equipment on board
(John Dodds Studios)

All lifeboats carry the RNLI 'house flag', designed in about 1884 by Miss Leonora Frances Margaret Preston, sister of a member of the Committee of Management. Lifeboats may also fly a Red Ensign with their house flag on it (behind RNLI flag in main photo).

Lifeboat crews are often called out in the worst weather conditions. Their protective clothing must be warm, waterproof and easily seen by crew and casualties alike. This lifeboatwoman wears a dry suit for entering the water to rescue a survivor.

Warming up with a hot drink

Lifeboats may be at sea for hours at a time. There is little time to think of eating, but survivors and lifeboat crews welcome a hot drink and a snack of chocolate or biscuits. The cans of food have their own heat source, which warms the food inside when activated.

The special RNLI lifejackets are designed to keep the wearer face-up in the water when inflated. Each one has a whistle and a light to alert rescuers.

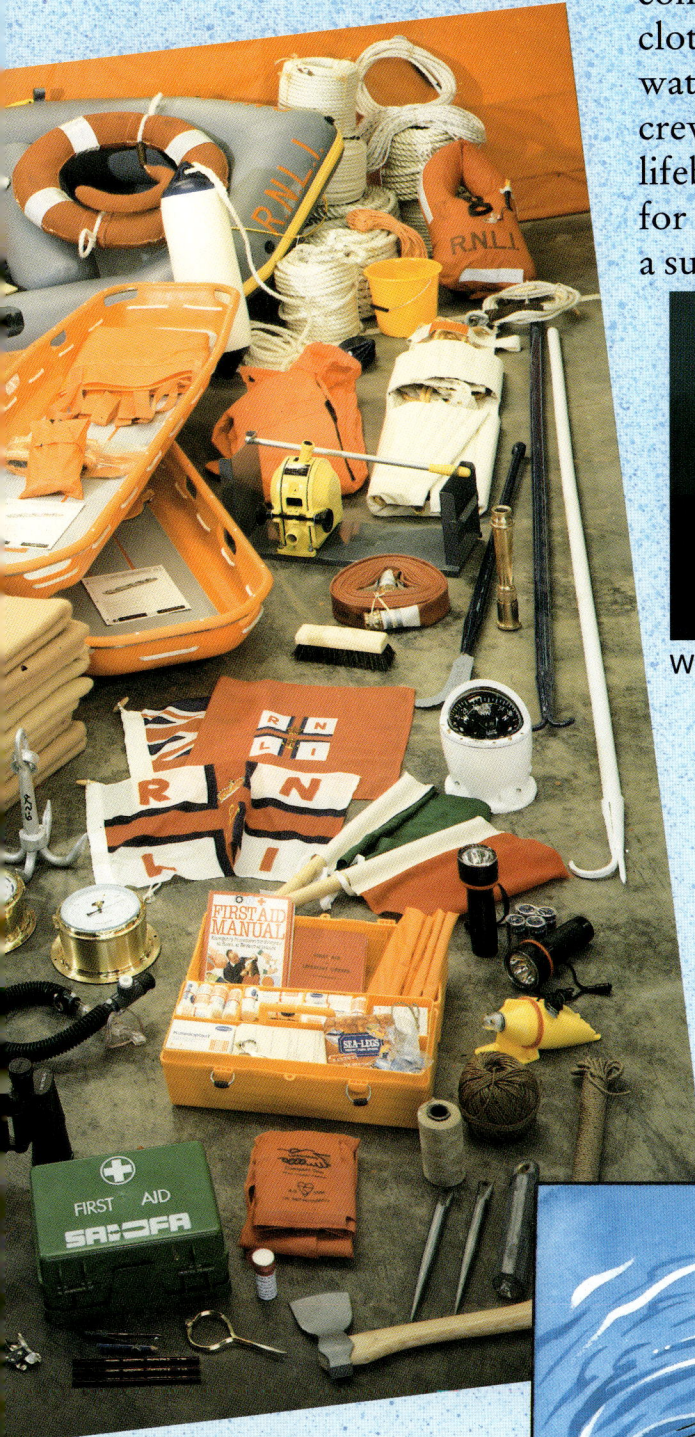

Rescue!

Since the RNLI was founded in 1824, its lifeboats have saved the lives of over 120,000 people. Nearly 5,000 calls for help were answered in 1990. That means an average of 13 lifeboat launches every day of the year. As you read these words, it is almost certain that a lifeboat is at sea on a rescue mission somewhere around the coast of Britain.

The stories on these pages highlight some of the emergencies that can arise at sea.

Towing the *Koo-She*
(Phil Shannon)

Disabled yacht

The Rother class Sennen Cove lifeboat was called out to a yacht drifting towards rocks in gale-force winds and heavy seas. A helicopter was also called out, but the lifeboat was able to reach the yacht, the *Koo-She*, just in time and tow her to safety. This dramatic picture was taken by crew member Phil Shannon during the four-hour tow to harbour.

The Waveney that saved the skin-divers
(Dave Trotter)

Fire at sea!

The Arun class lifeboat from Tynemouth was called out to a fishing vessel that had caught fire. Two crewmen from the fishing boat, the *Kalisto*, who had jumped overboard and been airlifted to safety, reported that there were gas cylinders on board and a danger of explosions. Crew members from the lifeboat risked their lives to go on board the blazing vessel and put out the fire.

Skin-divers rescued in Eyemouth's Waveney lifeboat
(Robin Sharp)

Divers in danger

Eyemouth's Waveney class lifeboat was called out in hurricane-force winds to the aid of two skin-divers. The lifeboat faced waves over ten metres high, and had great difficulty in finding the divers. A powercut on shore meant that car headlights had to be used to guide the lifeboat safely to shore again!

Shifting cargo

When cargo shifts, unbalancing the vessel that is carrying it, there is always danger – especially in gale-force winds. This is what happened to the Maltese cargo ship *Al Kwather 1* at anchor three and a half miles from shore. The Yarmouth (Isle of Wight) relief Arun class lifeboat rescued two men from the cargo ship in very dangerous conditions.

Rescuing the crew of *Al Kwather 1*

The coxswain and his crew

The size of the crew of a lifeboat varies, but the person in charge when the lifeboat is at sea is the **coxswain**. He makes many of the split second decisions that can save lives in danger.

The coxswain is chosen by the crew members themselves, as someone they can trust with their lives. The coxswain must know his boat and the waters of his coastline. He must be an excellent seaman. Above all, he must be able to help his crew grow into a team that works together when danger threatens.

The story below took place on 26 August 1989, when Teesmouth's relief Tyne-class lifeboat, the *RNLB Owen and Ann Aisher* was called to the aid of a fishing boat, the *Gang Warily*.

A coxswain in command
(David Trotter)

RNLI medals

For his courage and skill, Coxswain Peter Race was awarded the RNLI's bronze medal.

BUFFETED BY FORCE 7 WINDS AND 12 FOOT WAVES THE FISHING BOAT HAD GONE AGROUND... THERE WAS ONE COURSE OF ACTION FOR THE CREW....

ABANDON SHIP! MAKE FOR THOSE ROCKS!

REDCAR'S ATLANTIC 21 "LORD BROTHERTON" IS FIRST ON THE SCENE. SECURED BY A ROPE, CREWMAN **PETER LODGE** SWIMS TO SHORE – AS THE MEN ARE HAULED BACK–TRAGEDY STRIKES.

THE LINE'S FOULED– IT'S DRAGGING US UNDER – WE'VE GOT TO CUT OURSELVES FREE!

THE "OWEN AND ANN AISHER" ARRIVES BUT IS UNABLE TO GET WITHIN 150 FT. OF THE FISHERMEN.

WITH THE TIDE RISING FAST, THE STRICKEN MEN ARE IN GRAVE DANGER.... COXSWAIN **PETER RACE** DECIDES ON A BOLD COURSE OF ACTION....

WE'LL RUN A DINGHY IN ON THE WIND!

BATTERED AGAINST ROCKS, THE **"OWEN AND ANN AISHER"** MIRACULOUSLY HOLDS HER POSITION AND EDGES THE DINGHY TOWARDS THE TRAPPED MEN.

CRACK!

CLAMBERING ABOARD, INCH BY INCH THE MEN ARE DRAGGED THROUGH THE SURF TO SAFETY.

A coxswain may also be the mechanic of his lifeboat, or the mechanic may be another crew member. Being a mechanic on lifeboats over ten metres long is a full-time job, and the mechanic is a permanent employee of the RNLI. Otherwise, coxswains and crews take time from their own work for lifeboat training and duties, and are paid only a small contribution towards their expenses.

Where did the word 'coxswain' come from?

Often shortened to 'cox', it is thought that the word comes from two old English words: 'cog' (a small boat) and 'sweyne' (the man in charge).

chanic checking equipment
(s Fairclough)

Mobile training unit
(Edward Mallinson)

The RNLI awards gold, silver and bronze medals, as well as framed letters of thanks, written on vellum, for deeds of exceptional skill and bravery.

Crew in training

Running to a call

Crew members are trained by the coxswain and at special RNLI training sessions. They must be fit, interested in the sea and able to work well with other crew members.

At one time, maroons (signal rockets which explode in the air with a loud bang) were set off to call out the lifeboat crew. Today, crew members carry bleepers with them at all times.

World-wide rescue

The RNLI was the first nationally-organised lifeboat service in the world, but within months of its founding in 1824 other countries had begun to follow suit. The first of these was the lifeboat service of the Netherlands, which is run in a similar way to the RNLI.

The RNLI and the Dutch service have always had close links, but they are also in contact with nearly forty other lifeboat services from around the world. All these services are members of the International Lifeboat Federation (ILF).

Although ILF members have to deal with very different coastal and weather conditions, they are all dedicated to the same service – saving life at sea. They keep in close touch with each other and every four years meet at an international conference to discuss new life-saving equipment and methods.

Canada

USA

Bermuda

Bahamas
British Virgin
Islands
Netherlands
Antilles

Guatemala

Chile   Uruguay

Argentina

Iceland
Faro
Islar
N
United Kingdor
De
Netherla
Belgiur
Franc

Portugal   Spai

Morocco

Members of

A Clyde-class ex-RNLI boat is now used by Iceland both for life-saving and for training. Boats that are no longer needed by the RNLI often continue to play a useful role elsewhere.

Bermuda makes use of jet-propelled boats. These are needed where there are reefs or heavy surf that might damage propellers.

Jet propelled boat in Bermuda

Canada has to cope with extreme conditions around its coast in the winter. Boats and people may become trapped in or *on* the ice. Rescue needs to be very quick indeed if those at risk are to survive the cold.

Canadian lifeboat in ice
(Paul Heath)

The US coastguard runs the largest lifeboat service in the world, funded by the US government. It developed a boat that has seen service in many countries, including Britain. We know it as the Waveney.

US coastguard lifeboat

It may be a surprise that Switzerland is a member of the ILF because it has no sea coast at all. But about 75 Swiss lifeboats are kept busy on Lake Geneva.

Japan
China
Hong Kong
India
Turkey
South Africa
Australia
New Zealand
ational Lifeboat Federation

Inshore lifeboat in New Zealand

In New Zealand, several different organisations around the coast co-operate to save lives at sea. Inflatables like this one, pioneered by the French lifeboat service, are ideal for inshore rescue.

It takes a team

This picture shows just some of the people who make the life-saving work of the Hastings lifeboats possible. All lifeboat stations rely on a team of dedicated volunteers and professionals like this. Some of them have been highlighted on these pages, but all of them are vital to the continued success of the service.

The **Committee** of the lifeboat station is made up of local volunteers, standing here in front of the Mersey lifeboat, and is responsible for the day-to-day running of the station.

The **coxswains and crews** of the Mersey class lifeboat and the inflatable lifeboat are standing in the front of the picture. They spend long hours training and are always on call. Only the mechanic is a full-time employee of the RNLI.

The **Chairman of the Station Branch Committee**, seated in the centre of the picture, heads the committee that is responsible for the running of the station. The hard work of the committee ensures that no opportunity to increase awareness of the RNLI is missed.

(Campbell MacCullum)

Every lifeboat station has at least one **Medical Adviser**. The two doctors of the Hastings station are standing behind the bows of the inflatable. If necessary, they are prepared to go out with the lifeboat, facing the same dangers as the coxswain and crew.

Grouped around their vehicle, members of **HM Coastguard** play a vital role in co-ordinating rescue attempts. Often the first to be warned of a problem at sea, they keep in radio contact with the lifeboat and can call on helicopters or other vessels to help.

The **Honorary Secretary** of the committee, standing to the left behind the Branch Chairman, is alerted by the coastguard and makes the decision to send out the lifeboat. He or she (or a deputy) must be on call at all times.

The **Launching and Recovery Crew**, standing on and in front of the tractor that is used to launch and recover the lifeboat, may also be needed at any time of day or night.

Also in the picture are representatives of the **police, fire and ambulance** services. They work closely with the RNLI to ensure that casualties receive the best possible care at sea and ashore.

17

Unbeatable inflatables!

Since their introduction in 1963, inflatable lifeboats have proved their value – they are now involved in well over half the successful sea rescues every year. For inshore work, rescuing swimmers, windsurfers and small-boat sailors who get into difficulties, they are unbeatable.

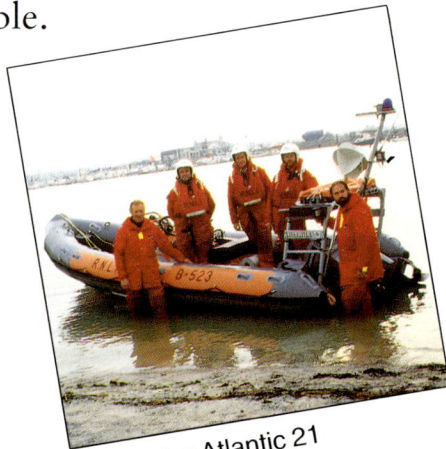
Blue Peter Atlantic 21

This Atlantic 21 and five other inflatables were funded by *Blue Peter* viewers. The Atlantic 21 has a rigid hull with an inflated tube round the top called a **sponson.** This makes it faster and more stable than other inflatables. It is also able to be self-righted.

The advantages of inflatables are that they are:
- quick to launch
- fast in the water
- very manoeuvrable
- able to operate in shallow water

The students of Atlantic College, South Wales, have their own lifeboat station. The founder of the school, Admiral Desmond Hoare, helped to develop a rigid-hulled inflatable in the early 1960s. The average age of the crew is 18.

Any lifeboat can be uncomfortable in bad weather, but the gymnastic leaps of the inflatables can give crews a real jolting!

For this reason, the age limit for crews is 45 – 10 years younger than that for other boats.

Take a closer look at the 'D' class inflatable. Notice the way that the tubes are divided into sections so that if one is punctured the boat will still float.

Inflatable fact file

	Length	Speed	Station fleet	Relief fleet
Atlantic 21	6.9 m	29 knots (33 mph)	45	22
'C' Class	5.3 m	27 knots (31 mph)	12	5
'D' Class	4.9 m	20 knots (23 mph)	84	37

Inflatable fighting rough seas
(Ian Bardell)

By carrying an inflatable for launch at sea, some all-weather lifeboats increase their flexibility in different rescue situations.

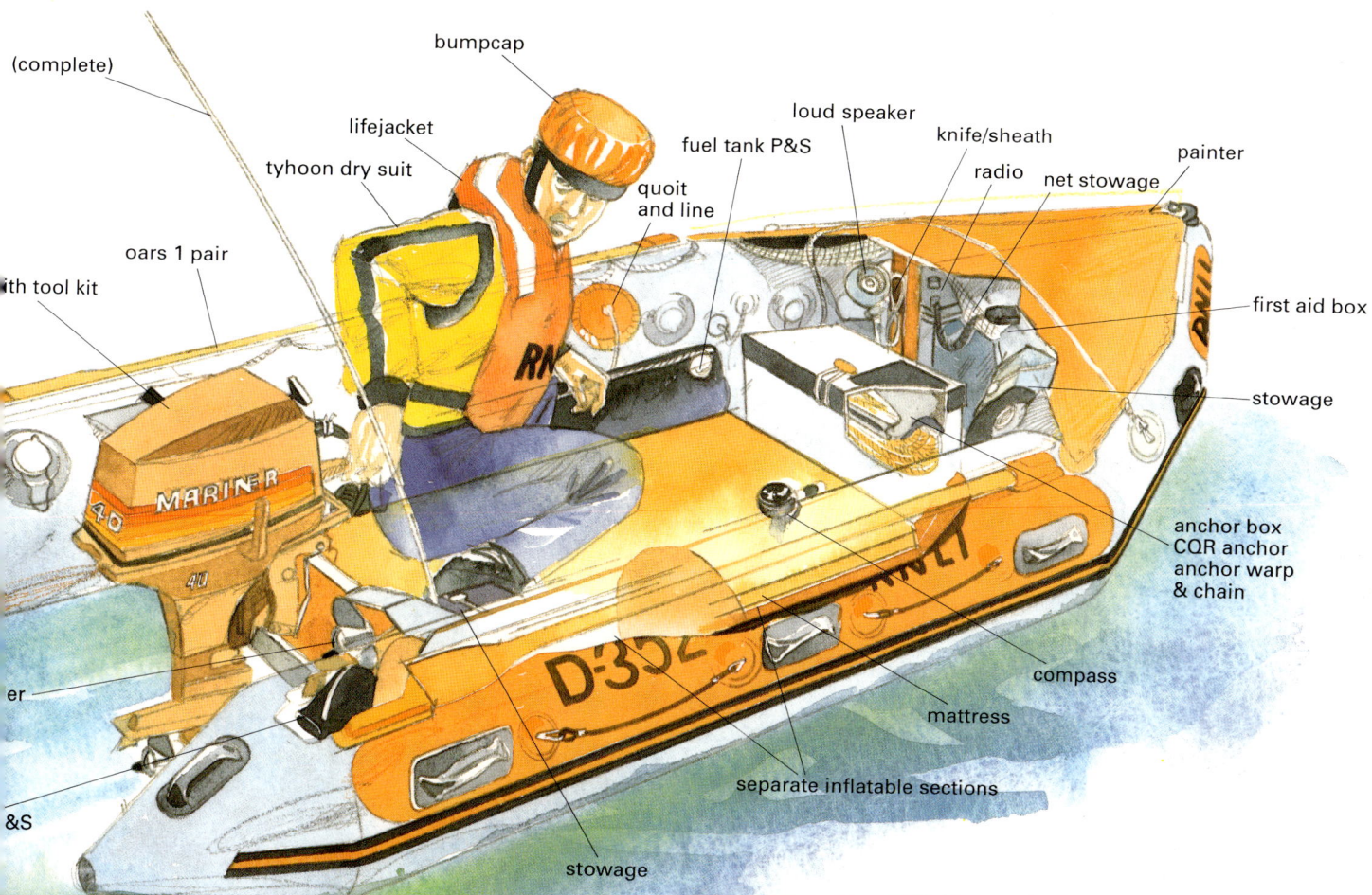

(complete)

bumpcap

lifejacket

loud speaker

knife/sheath

painter

tyhoon dry suit

fuel tank P&S

radio

net stowage

quoit and line

oars 1 pair

first aid box

ith tool kit

stowage

MARINER

40

40

anchor box
CQR anchor
anchor warp
& chain

D-352

RNLI

compass

er

mattress

&S

separate inflatable sections

stowage

All-weather action

Although inflatables are ideal for inshore work, rescues up to fifty miles from shore or in bad weather demand the power and safety of an all-weather lifeboat.

An all-weather lifeboat requires:
- speed and power
- manoeuvrability
- reliability
- self-righting ability

(Malory Maltby)

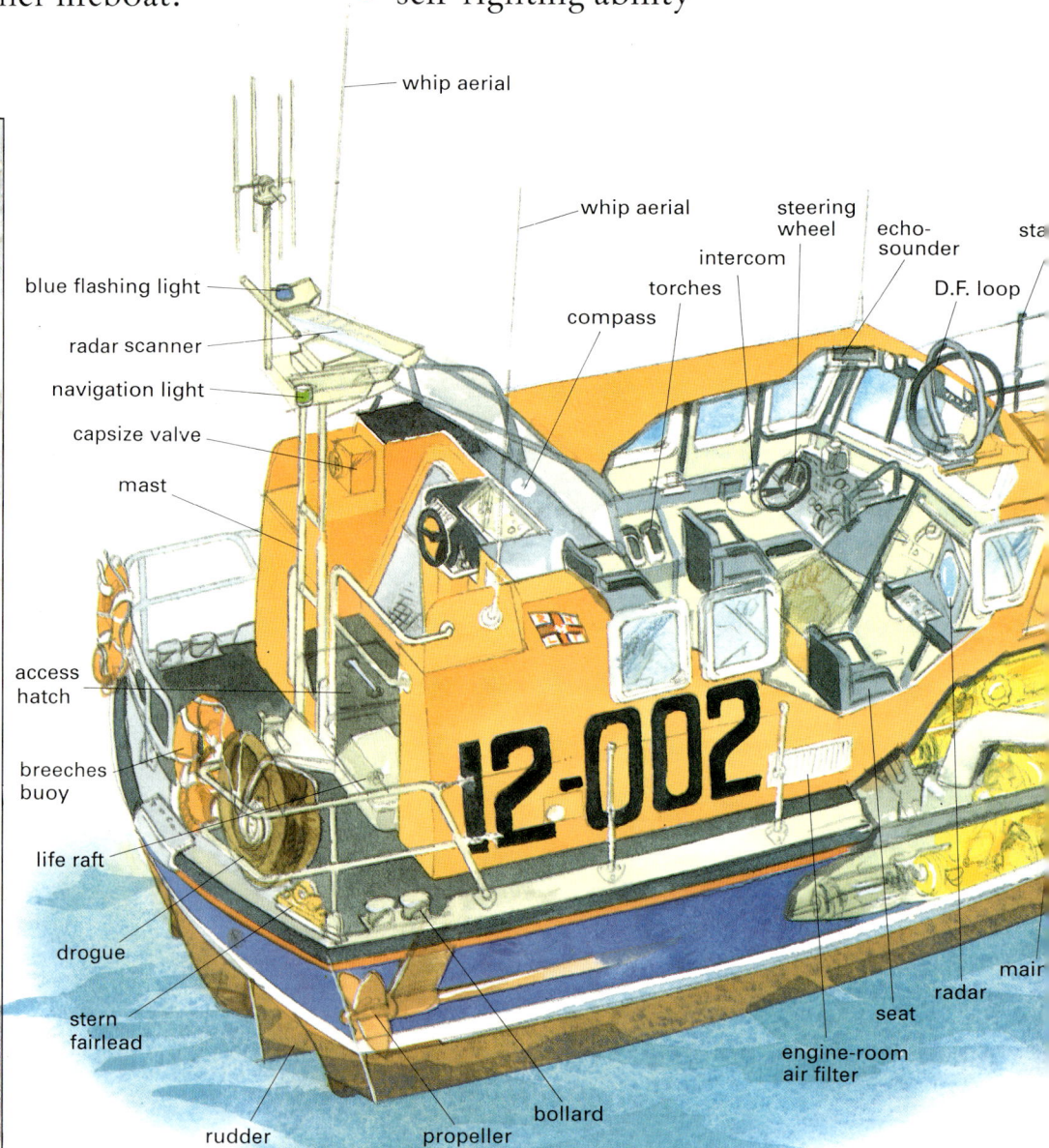

whip aerial

whip aerial

steering wheel

echo-sounder

sta

intercom

D.F. loop

torches

blue flashing light

compass

radar scanner

navigation light

capsize valve

mast

access hatch

breeches buoy

life raft

12-002

drogue

stern fairlead

mair

radar

seat

engine-room air filter

rudder

propeller

bollard

Most all-weather lifeboats have a crew of six or seven. All lifeboats over 10 metres long have a full-time mechanic. The careful maintenance they receive means that the life span of an all-weather lifeboat averages 20 to 30 years, despite the rough conditions they often meet.

Over the years, the design of the all-weather boat has changed enormously, and the RNLI continues to develop new boats using the very latest technology.

Mersey lifeboat in action
(Ambrose Greenway)

The Mersey class lifeboat is the most recent to have come into service. A carriage-launched lifeboat, it was designed to replace the traditional Rother and Oakley classes. A vigorous building programme means that Merseys will have replaced the slower boats by early 1993.

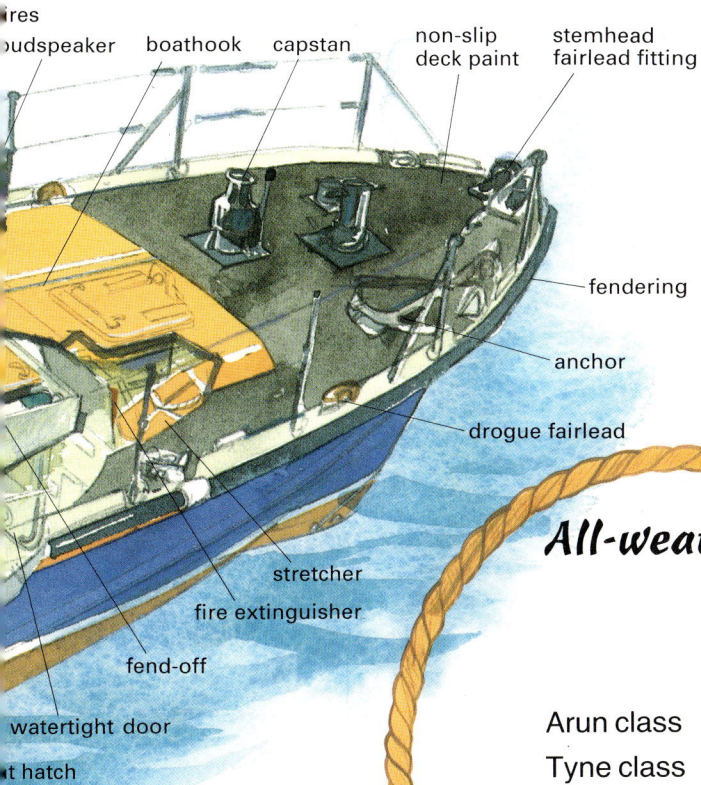

loudspeaker boathook capstan non-slip deck paint stemhead fairlead fitting

fendering

anchor

drogue fairlead

stretcher

fire extinguisher

fend-off

watertight door

hatch

All-weather fact file

	Length	Speed	Station fleet	Relief fleet
Arun class	15.9/16.5 m	18.2 knots (21 mph)	37	9
Tyne class	14.3 m	17.6 knots (20 mph)	34	6
Mersey class	11.6 m	17 knots (20 mph)	14	3
Waveney class	13.4 m	15.4 knots (18 mph)	14	8
Thames class	15.2 m	17.5 knots (20 mph)	2	0
Brede class	10.0 m	18.6 knots (21 mph)	5	3
Solent class	14.8 m	9.25 knots (11 mph)	4	2
Oakley class	11.3 m	8 knots (9 mph)	10	8
Rother class	11.4 m	8 knots (9 mph)	9	5

Launch and recovery

It seems obvious that lifeboats have to be launched and recovered, but it's not as easy as it sounds. Lifeboats have to be ready to go out at any time – they can't wait hours for the tide to rise or fall. Many helpers may be needed to get the lifeboat afloat. Bringing her safely home can be even more difficult.

A slipway launch is fast and efficient where there are cliffs or no sheltered harbour. Recovering the lifeboat is much more difficult. A cable has to be attached to the stern and the boat winched back up the slipway. In bad weather it may be hours before this can be done.

The wide beach at Aldeburgh means that the lifeboat has to be launched down a short slipway and then across skids into the sea.
(Jeff Morris)

Carriage launch
(Ambrose Greenway)

On parts of the coast where there is a wide sandy beach at low tide, the lifeboat has to be dragged in and out of the sea on a carriage. Special waterproof tractors have been

developed to push the carriages into deep water. Recovery is harder. The lifeboat is dragged on skids up the beach to her carriage, which tilts backwards to let her on.

It may seem that lifeboats that lie at moorings have an easier time. But in very rough weather the trip out to the lifeboat by boarding boat can be tricky, and there is no boathouse to protect the lifeboat or those who work on her.

Small inflatables are carried by Arun and Tyne lifeboats and are launched at sea.

Until the 1930s, horses were a common means of launching and recovering lifeboats.

Atlantic 21 on a trolley

Smaller inflatables can be launched on trolleys pushed by only a few people. The larger Atlantic 21 has her engines running and is literally driven off her launching trolley by the helmsman.

At Aldeburgh, the shingle shifts too much to allow carriage launching. Helpers drag the lifeboat over skids placed on the beach, often getting cold and wet in the process.

Aldeburgh lifeboat

Back to the drawing board

The RNLI fleet is being updated constantly, developing to meet changing requirements and to take advantage of new technology. The most recent lifeboats to be designed are the new **Fast Afloat Boats**, known as FAB3 and FAB4. The plan is that they will eventually replace the Arun and Waveney classes.

The first stage in designing a new lifeboat is to decide what is needed from the boat. The RNLI came up with a long list of requirements, and some of the most important were:

- a maximum speed of at least 25 knots;
- a protected propeller for use in shallow water;
- a boat that is easy to maintain.

The RNLI designers went to work in their drawing office at RNLI headquarters in Poole.

How are new classes of lifeboat named?

You may have noticed that recent all-weather lifeboats have been named after rivers. It is planned that this will continue. What would be your choices for the new FAB3 and FAB4 boats?

To make sure that the hull shape was correct, models of the designs were tested both in a tank and at sea.

Any new lifeboat has to undergo thorough trials. Here the prototype FAB3, built in **FRC** (Fibre Reinforced Composite) is being deliberately capsized to make sure that she rights herself within seconds.

FAB3 has a yellow superstructure instead of the usual orange one. Experts think that yellow may be easier to see at long distances. If this is found to be the case, the whole RNLI fleet may eventually be painted yellow with blue hulls.

FAB fact file

	FAB3	FAB4
Length	17.0 m	14.0 m
Max. speed	25 knots (29 mph)	25 knots (29 mph)
Crew	5/6	5/6
Survivors carried	up to 20	up to 10
Time at sea	up to 10 hours	up to 10 hours

Whatever the weather . . .

It has become rather a joke that people talk about the weather when they don't know what else to say. But at sea the weather is no joke.

Inexperienced sailors feel safe when the sea is calm, but a change can come very quickly.

Winds are caused by air moving from an area of high pressure to an area of lower pressure. You can often feel this happening when you are by the sea. Air cooling and sinking over the sea increases the pressure, while air rising over the warm land lowers the pressure. A sea breeze results where they meet.

Whipped by the winds, the sea can be a tremendously destructive force. (Robin Sharp)

A boat can often ride quite large waves if it is pointing into them, but a wave hitting the side of the boat can capsize it. Many lifeboats carry a **drogue** – a heavy canvas tube that can be trailed behind the boat to keep it at right angles to the waves.

Lifeboat dragging a drogue (Peter Hadfield)

Sailors have some help in predicting bad weather from the radio shipping forecasts. You may have wondered where such places as 'Fisher' and 'Bailey' are. This map shows that they are simply areas of sea.

You may think that only crews in sailing boats need to worry about the strength of the wind. But it is the wind blowing along the surface of the sea that causes waves, and heavy seas can be dangerous to any vessel.

The **Beaufort Wind Scale** is used to describe the strength of the wind.

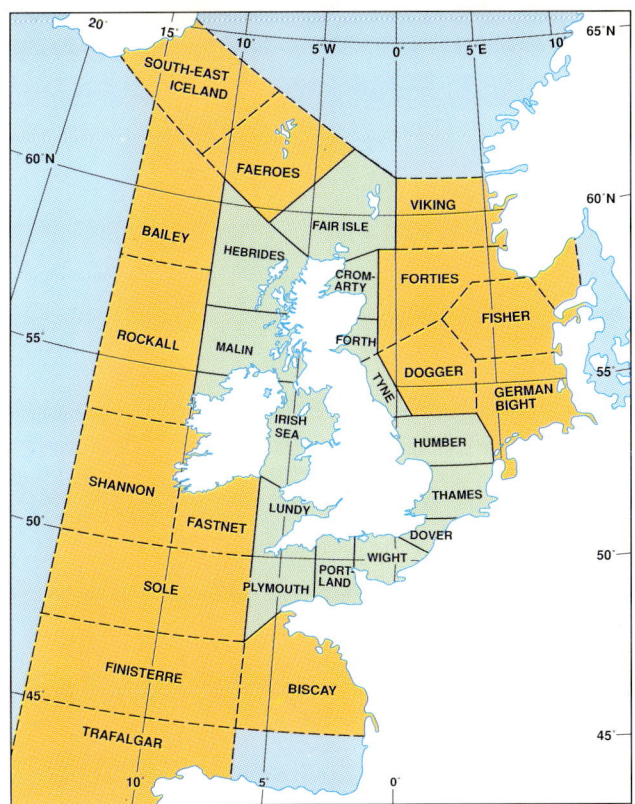

0 Calm

1 Light air

2 Light breeze

3 Gentle breeze

4 Moderate breeze

5 Fresh breeze

6 Strong breeze

7 Near gale

8 Gale

9 Strong gale

10 Storm

11 Violent storm

12 Hurricane

It seems as though waves move water forward, but in fact they move it round in a kind of circle.

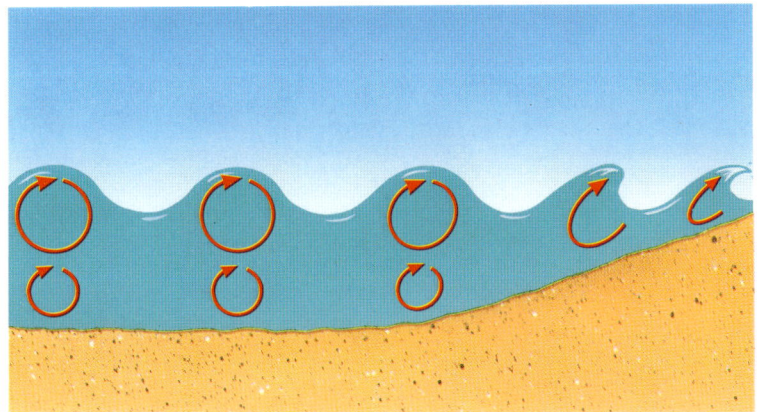

Have you heard of the expression 'spreading oil on troubled waters'? Some lifeboats can do just that! They carry non-polluting fish oil that can be released into the sea. The oil floats on the surface and temporarily flattens the waves.

(John Dodds Studios)

Did you know?

Lifeboat crews would agree that a lifetime is not long enough to learn all there is to know about the sea and saving lives in danger. But here are some answers to a few of the things you may have wondered about.

Each lifeboat has a distinctive number

How fast is a knot?

A knot is a speed of one nautical mile per hour. It is so called because sailors used to trail a knotted rope through the water to work out a boat's speed. How far is a nautical mile? It's 1,853.18 metres! To work out what a speed in knots is in miles-per-hour, multiply it by 1.15.

What do the numbers on the side of a lifeboat mean?

The first set of numbers show the lifeboat's length in feet or, for newer boats, in metres. The following numbers show whether this was the first, third or twenty-third boat of that class to be built. What can you tell about this boat?

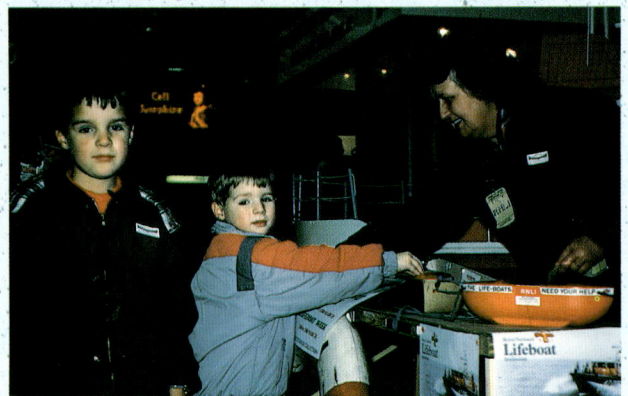

How much does a lifeboat cost?

Modern lifeboats have all the latest equipment to help crews to save lives – and that equipment is expensive. A new Mersey class lifeboat costs £650,000 to build. The Fast Afloat Boats under development at the moment, will cost £1,000,000. The RNLI needs all the fundraising support you can give it.

Fund-raising for the RNLI (Robin Sharp)

Who chooses the name of a lifeboat?

It depends. Usually, if an organisation or a person has given over half the money for a lifeboat (and that's a lot of money!) they have the right to name it. So you will see lifeboats named after people, cities and companies. This photograph shows the naming ceremony of RNLB *Marine Engineer*.

(Robin Sharp)

Do lifeboat crews ever get seasick?

Yes! Sometimes conditions are so bad that even the most experienced lifeboatman is sick.

Will helicopters take over from lifeboats?

No. Helicopters are very important in many rescue attempts, and the Royal Navy works closely with the RNLI, but they will never take over completely. Lifeboats can stay at sea much longer and can go out in weather that keeps the helicopters on the ground.

RN helicopter in exercise with a lifeboat

Into the future

Early motor lifeboat

It comes as a shock to realise that there was a time when there was no help at all for sailors who were shipwrecked.

After one dreadful shipwreck in 1789, Newcastle businessmen offered a prize for the best design for a lifeboat. The result was Henry Greathead's *The Original*.

William Hillary

Greathead's Original

The first lifeboat day

The first motor-powered lifeboats, introduced in 1904, soon proved their usefulness.

In 1891 Sir Charles Macara organised the first ever charity street collection in Manchester in aid of lifeboats – the very first Lifeboat Day.

An Atlantic 21

Prototype FAB3
(Edward Mallinson)

The introduction of inflatables in 1963 revolutionised the speed and manoeuvrability of inshore lifeboats.

The RNLI never ceases to develop new, improved lifeboats. Two Fast Afloat Boats (FABs) are now being developed.

In 1824 a National Institution for the Preservation of Life from Shipwreck was set up following the plans of Sir William Hillary.

In 1838 the public's attention was caught by the dramatic rescue of nine men, women and children by Grace Darling and her father off the Farne Islands.

Grace Darling

In 1851 the Duke of Northumberland announced a new competition for lifeboat design. The winner was a self-righting lifeboat which formed the basis of the fleet for the next 50 years.

The first steam-powered lifeboat was built in 1890 and was very successful.

Since 1869 the Institution has been funded entirely by voluntary contributions. The RNLI is proud to continue this tradition.

First steam lifeboat

Fund-raising (Robin Sharp)

Today, as in the past, it is the people of Britain and Ireland who give the RNLI all the support it needs. Turn the page to find one way that *you* can help . . .

Over to you

Would you like regular updates on the latest amazing rescues, more information about lifeboats, and the chance to be in touch with RNLI supporters all around the country? Why not join Storm Force, a club for anyone under sixteen with an interest in lifeboats? And you'll be helping to support the RNLI too!

New members receive a pack containing a membership certificate, badge, poster, stickers and a copy of Storm Force News. This colourful magazine is packed with the latest information about rescue, lifeboats and the activities of RNLI crews and supporters, as well as puzzles, cartoons and competitions. It will be sent to you four times each year.

Storm Force member naming a train

To join, send a cheque or postal order for £3.00 (made out to the RNLI) with a note of your name, address and date of birth to: Storm Force HQ, RNLI, West Quay Road, Poole, Dorset BH15 1HZ.

Your club or class can join Storm Force as a group so long as there are at least ten of you. Send £1.00 for each member in a cheque or postal order and don't forget to give an address for the group. You'll each receive a membership certificate, badge and stickers, and your group will get two copies of Storm Force News to share.

Storm Force member Laura Scaife won the chance to name an Intercity 125 train after her club in a Storm Force competition.

Index

Acknowledgments
The author and publisher would like to thank the following for permission to reproduce photographic material in this book: Ian Bardell, John Dodds Studios, Chris Fairclough, Ambrose Greenway, Peter Hadfield, Paul Heath, Campbell MacCullum, Edward Mallinson, Malory Maltby, Jeff Morris, Phil Shannon, Robin Sharp, David Trotter, Tony Vandervell and the RNLI..
© 1992 Nicola Baxter

This hardback edition published 1993 by Watts Books
96 Leonard Street
London
EC2A 4RH

Franklin Watts Australia
14 Mars Road
Lane Cove
NSW 2066

ISBN 0 7496 1311 4
Dewey Decimal Classification 387.5

A CIP record is available from the British Library

10 9 8 7 6 5 4 3 2 1

First published in the United Kingdom in 1992 by Hodder & Stoughton Ltd